Animal Tricks

Jan Burchett and Sara Vogler

Houghton Mifflin Harcourt.

Contents

Animal Tricks was originally published in English in 2016. This edition is published by arrangement with Oxford University Press.

Printed in China

ISBN 978-0-358-26187-2

1 2 3 4 5 6 7 8 9 10 XXXX 28 27 26 25 24 23 22 21 20 19

4500000000 A B C D E F G

Inside cover notes written by Karra McFarlane

Acknowledgments

Series Editor: Nikki Gamble

The publisher would like to thank the following for permission to reproduce photographs: **Cover&p11:** Danita Delimont/Alamy; **back cover&p12f:** Ogphoto/ Istockphoto; **p1,p6,p8,p12&p16:** Shutterstock; **p3:** Mjarnold87/ Dreamstime; **p4:** Craig Dingle/Istockphoto; **p5:** Vladimir Sazonov/ Shutterstock; **p6:** Joel Sartore/GettyImages; **p7:** Aquanaut4/ Dreamstime. com; **p8&p16:** Georgette Douwma/Nature Picture Library; **p9:** Roger Meets/ Shutterstock; **p10t:** kuritafsheen/Getty Images; **p10b:** Shutterstock; **p12a:** Buddy Mays/Corbis; **p12b:** Kim Taylor/Getty Images; **p12c:** Survivalphotos; **p12d:** WILDLIFE GmbH; **p12e:** John Cancalosi/Nature Picture Library; **p13:** Jennifer Hayes/Getty Images; **p14b:** Tolga TEZCAN/Istockphoto; **p15:** Denis Scott/Fuse/Getty Images; **p16:** Mathisa/Shutterstock

Houghton Mifflin Harcourt Publishing Company
125 High Street
Boston, MA 02110
www.hmhco.com

Is It a Tree?

What is it?
Is it a tree?

No, it's a trick!
It is a bird.

It looks like a tree. It can sneak up on its dinner without being seen.

Is It a Snake?

What is it? Is it a snake?

No, it's a trick! It is a moth. Its **wing tips** help to frighten its attackers.

Is It a Fish?

What is it? Is it a fish?

No, it's a trick! It is an octopus.

It's pretending to be a fish
that can hurt attackers.

Is It a Flower?

What is it?
Is it a flower?

No, it’s a trick! This is a mantis. It is a big **insect**.

Little insects think the mantis is a flower and land on it. The mantis eats little insects.

Is It an Owl?

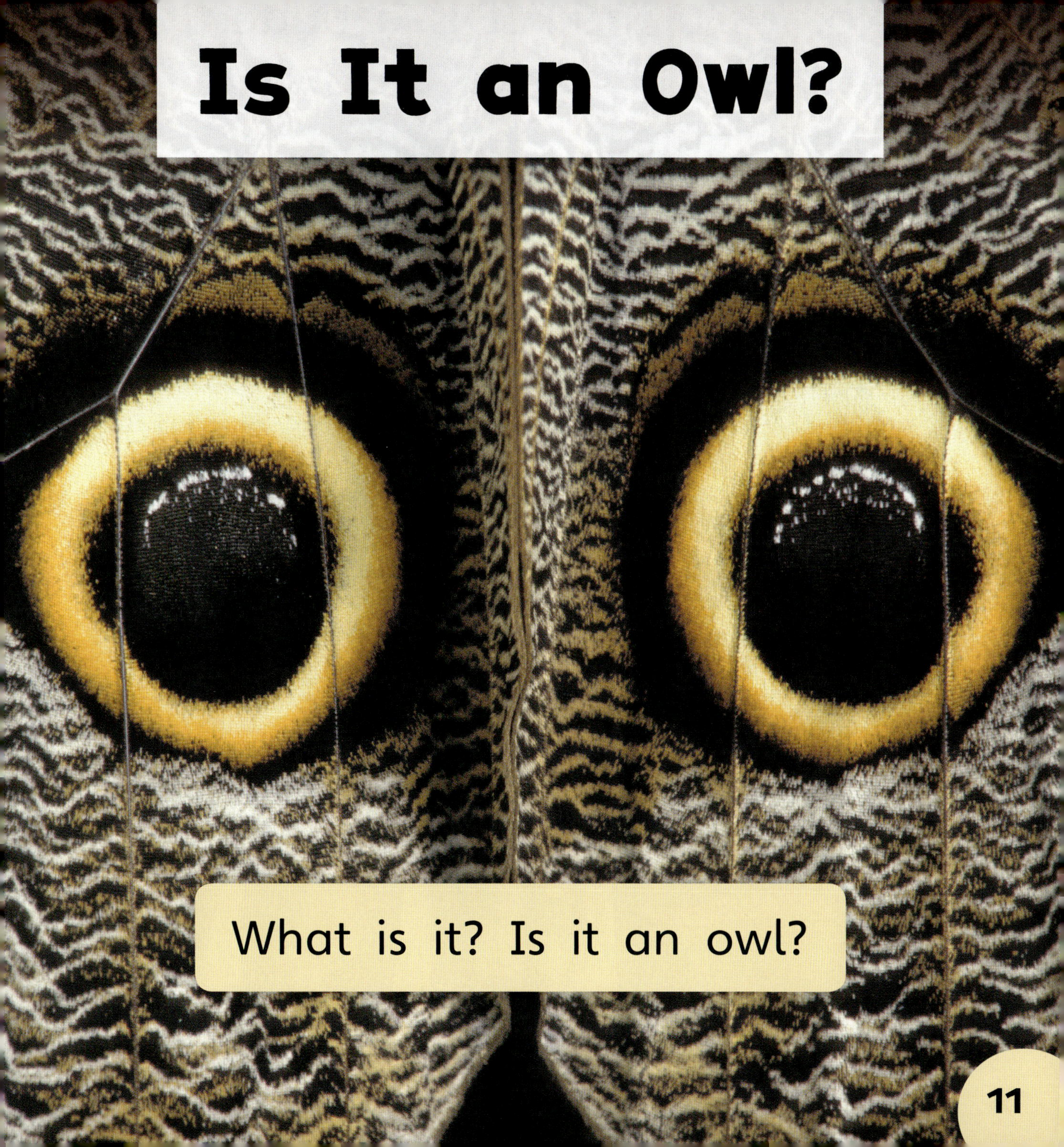

What is it? Is it an owl?

No, it's a trick! It is a butterfly.
Attackers think it's an owl.
This frightens them off.

What Is It?

Is it a fish?
Or is it a trick?

It's not a trick! It is a shark.
A shark is a big fish.

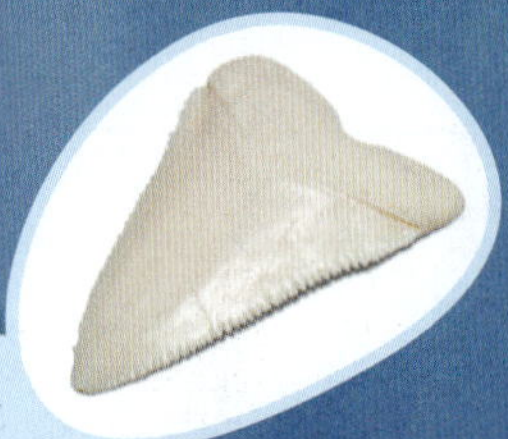

Sharks have big, sharp teeth
so they do not need tricks!

I need my dinner!

Glossary

antenna: a thin feeler on an insect

insect: a little animal with six legs

wing tips: the ends of an animal's wings

Index